Samuel Johnson

Belshazzar's Doom

Samuel Johnson

Belshazzar's Doom

ISBN/EAN: 9783743332089

Manufactured in Europe, USA, Canada, Australia, Japa

Cover: Foto ©ninafisch / pixelio.de

Manufactured and distributed by brebook publishing software
(www.brebook.com)

Samuel Johnson

Belshazzar's Doom

Belshazzar's Doom.

COMPOSED BY

SAMUEL JOHNSON.

ST. PAUL, MINN.
1887.

Printed by Wanderer Printing Co.
St. Paul, Minn.

BELSHAZZAR'S DOOM.

A kiug there lived in ancient ages
Who did possess a wondrous fame; ·
Not Solomon the sage of sages;—
This was another king by name
Belshazzar, and still history's pages
Tell of his life, his death, his shame,
His heavy sins and their high wages,
And how he played a fatal game.

He ruled o'er mighty Babylon, the famous,
The loveliest of cities in the world,
The kingdom which o'er other ancient kingdoms
The banner of supremacy unfurled.
He was Nebuchadnezzar's son and scion,—
His very image in all wicked ways;
He lived as independent as the lion
And won through sin and vice the wicked's praise.

He ruled his monarchy with rods of iron,
And when enraged the flames of wrath would blaze
Until they reached to heav'n, to God of Zion,
Who even now was numbering his days.

But never did he lift his eyes to heaven
And therefore could not see a higher pow'r;
He was himself monarch; who could tell him
A king above him had him in his pow'r?
No time for this! a king, a brute, a tyrant
Has other things than these to keep in mind,
For he must rule as he is ruled by Satan!
A vassal and a king are here combin'd!

But often would he thirst for some amusement
And let the tyrant spirit take a rest,—
But this would never check his proud ambition;
The same vile heart still beat within his breast;
In kingly robes and state and pomp and glory
He hid his foul iniquities and shame:

Fair fortune smiled her sweetest on his kingdom,
With grand success she fed ambition's flame,—
But haughtiness and pride and vile ambition,
On which the lofty fly as tho' on wings,
According to the King's of Heav'n decision
Has ever been, and shall, the bane of kings!

And thus it is that mighty men
So often play the fool;
In their ascent they imitate
The mount'neer's heedless mule, —
They climb on unsafe footing
To the mountain's highest crown,
And never think that when they fall
It is a great way down.
Thus, did he climb on stepping stones
Of haughtiness and pride
"To higher realms" he thought, but no!
By One he was defied!
The One who ruled the realms above

Had fix'd his utmost height:
"Thus far, no farther shalt thou soar,
Vain eagle in thy flight!"
The King of kings was even now,
Although to him unknown,
Above his head and reaching forth
To hurl him from his throne!

The city long by foes had been surrounded,
The Medes' and Persians' formidable ranks
Had met the anxious gaze of Babylon's sentinels
Upon the hills and on the river's banks,
And round the walls, from dark Euphrates' entrance
E'en to its exit on the other side,
The foe's grim front was stationed like a death watch
Round those grim walls which even death defied.

King Cyrus with his great, tremendous army
Of Persian horsemen, forty-thousand strong,
And Lydian warriors well equipped and armed,

Of Phrygian javelin-men a massive throng,

And therewith scythed chariots and steeds,

The Coppadocians, by him subdued,

Who now had joined as allies to the Medes:

Arabian slingers in a multitude

On every side stood ready for the battle.

Must not such formidable foe cause dread? ·

An awful body, made to deal destruction,

But waits command from Cyrus, from its head.

He ranged his mighty forces round the walls,

But as he round the city spurred his steed

Lo! an Assyrian traitor doth approach!

Expecting to deserve a bounteous meed,

To Cyrus he imparts the secret minds,

The plans of those within the foe's defense,

And thus he speaks: "O Cyrus, be not rash!

Th' Assyrians show no signs of diffidence;

They laugh and mock your army, for they say

As from the walls your forces they survey,

Your chances do appear to them but weak;—
But this is what I would to thee convey:
They dare not come without the walls to fight
(For such an act would bring them sure defeat).
They'll keep in hiding till the danger's o'er;
But watch the treacherous lion, be discreet!
Gaze in his eyes and he will do no harm:
His courage then will fail — he will not stir;
Thus are these Babylonians, mark my word
That you no needless danger may incur,
For when you turn your forces to depart,
From yonder walls they'll open an attack;
Therefore, be on your watch, guard your retreat;
Like cowards they will turn upon your back!

Accepting this good counsel, Cyrus gives
His orders for retreat. The army then
In solid ranks move slowly from the scene.
Anon, they turn and face the foe again,
And thus they march; with face toward the wall,

They keep an eagle eye upon the foe,
Until safe distance guards them from the shafts,
The slings and arrows of the lurking foe:
Then, on they march till out of Babylon's view,
Nor halt until they reach their rendezvous.

The thoughtful general summons then around him
His most important officers to council,
Among whom were, Gobryas, an Assyrian
Whose son by King Belshazzar had been slain,
Gadatas, an Assyrian by birth.
Who also by this villain had been wronged,
And both, now thirsting to avenge their wrongs,
Had turned against Belshazzar, Babylon's king,
And joined with Cyrus, his most deadly foe,
To pay the bloody tyrant for their wrongs.
These officers and one by name Chrysantas
Composed the three most weighty men in council.

First Cyrus spoke: "Allies and friends,
Great difficulty this our plan attends:
We've viewed the city's stronghold round about,
And frankly, our success I greatly doubt!
Such massive walls we cannot take by force,—
We must pursue some more expedient course:
More plans than one I might indeed suggest,
And yet it seems to me a siege were best;
Let soldiers guard the city round about
And piercing famine soon will drive them out.
I think this is our plan to take our foes
Unless some better method you'd propose."
Chrysantas says: "Can we not ford the stream?"
Gobryas answers: "No, we'll never dream
Of such an undertaking, for my lord,
The river here is twice too deep to ford."
But Cyrus speaks: "No more Chrysantas! hold!
And hark to me while I my plan unfold:
Our force shall be arranged in three detachments,
And where Euphrates in the city

Be one detachment of the army stationed,

Another where the river makes its exit;

The third withdraw with me a little distance

Further up the river, to that place

Where Nitocris, once Babylon's famous queen,

Once turned the modest river from its bed:

There we will pierce the banks and force the flood

Out of its natural course in a canal

Which passes to that lake above the city

Which this same Nitocris, the queen, hath sunk.

Both forces then be vigilant and ready:

Be on your guard and watch the sinking stream:

When from the flood enough has been extracted,

That ye may possible effect an entrance,

Press forward, lose no time but march at once:

The river's bed shall be your line of march:

Both armies enter neath the massive walls

And meet within Belshazzar's battlements,

And there we'll join our forces all in one.

If we shall meet again within those walls

And force the brazen gates within to yield,
Belshazzar's power is but a fickle thing,
And short his reign as Babylon's mighty king!
We'll have him now — our plans he shall not foil!
But we must work: the steps to reach the throne
Are not yet built; 'tis but a night of toil,
And every man shall reap what he has sown!
Play well your parts, lose not a single cue;
Be brave as lions, sly as th' wary fox:
Your minds with thoughts of victory imbue,
And rest not till within Belshazzar's locks!
This very night the serpent must be slain,
For if he live uncertain is our gain:—
And let us swear tomorrow's rising sun
Must see the tyrant dead and th' castle won!"
Up from the secret conclave gathered there
The solemn oath swells on the midnight air
And in a murmur dies away: "We swear!"

Now Babylon thinks from danger she is free!
In blissful ignorance the people see,

Where there was no defeat, a victory:
They little dream what dangers hover near!
With joy they see the enemy disappear:
Pride and defiance take the place of fear.

For Babylon, by enemies surrounded,
Was threatened with destruction for a time;
But now the bells of liberty had sounded,
And all hearts swelled with joy to hear their chime!
The dreadful siege had reached its termination,
The enemy, a weary of suspense,
Had turned their backs, despairing an invasion
Into a castle with so strong defense.

So now the flags of liberty were flying,
The emblems of a peaceful victory,
All hearts are full of joy, no time for sighing,
For mighty Babylon again is free!

To celebrate their liberty,
Belshazzar made a festival,

A royal, grand reception
Unto his princes, dukes and lords.
And all without exception
Were invited by his honor at
This banquet to be present,
To revel in his luxuries
And spent the night so pleasant;
        would feast and revel
And pass the glorious time
In praising loud their sovereign,
The royal, the sublime!

The night is clear, the gentle zephyrs sigh
The branches of the lofty trees among;
The sprightly birds their evening lays have sung;
A cloud is cradled near the setting sun,
Its parting rays in splendor to increase,
A long, eventful day is almost done,
All nature prophesies a night of peace.

The princes, dukes and lords and mighty men
Begin to 'semble at the palace then,
The fluent orators and famous bards,
To sound his praise and pay their due regards;
The wise, the witty who could entertain,
The brightest fools within Belshazzar's reign,
The gayest women, bright society's lights,
Came to adorn the feast upon that night;
The great and greater gather side by side
With mingled love and malice, hate and pride.

The light of day ebbs, ebbs away;
The night comes swiftly on
And still the mass of revelers
Keeps surging, surging on.

The moon ascended to her throne
In heaven's dome so high,
And ushered out the myriad stars
In azure tinted sky.

Torch-light processions form in line
And march from street to street;
The crowds with songs and joyous shouts
Their dazzling glories greet.

The flames of bonfires leap to heaven,
Chaldea's dark sky to meet,
As to defy the stars with them
In glory to compete.

Against such odds, it seems to them,
The orbs of heav'n grow pale
As on the dark blue sea of sky
Far o'er the scene they sail!

The moon pales at the gorgeous sight,
As she gazes on the scene; —
The King of heaven veils her view
And hides her gentle sheen.

Across the spangled canopy
He draws the leaden clouds,
And wraps the hills and valleys round
In night's mysterious shrouds.

Ah! what a grand array of braves
Now throng the streets; behold!
When battle's wrinkled brow is smoothed
How Babylon grows bold!
The soldiers, gaily dressed and armed
With implements of war,
Parade the streets, and laugh and shout,
For danger is afar!

This is a night for Babylon
To worship golden gods,
To sing the glory of their king —
And kiss his iron rods!

No songs of joy or voice of thanks
To heavens King they raise:
But all in one united choir
To Satan's imp give praise.

Ten thousand voices fill the air
And make the echoes ring:
"Hail to our mighty sovereign,
Belshazzar, noble king!"

The merry songs, the shouts of praise
Reach to an earthly throne,
Then, empty honors, fall like chaff
By th' ruthless weather blown.

Belshazzar takes his royal seat,
The palace portals open wide,
And soon the scenes upon the streets
Resemble th' ebbing of the tide.

When the dim moon-light
Barely gilds the night,
Beware the enemy of light:
The tumult of day
Has died away
And now the devil seeks his prey.

The curtain rolls up on a dazzling scene,
One scarcely believes it but thinks it a dream;
The palace is seen with its spacious halls,
Its massive, decorated walls
Emblazoned with riches from near and from far,—
The trophies of battles, the relics of war,
The carvings, the sculptures of kings and of lords
Arrayed in their armour, with helmets and swords;
In the midst of the glory the sovereign's throne
Is set like in jewel the diamond stone,
Where in royal state and costly gown,
Belshazzar sits 'neath his heavy crown.

Sweet amazons, arrayed in costumes gay,
Like fairies to th' enchanting music sway:
Their eyes are lustrous as the luscious wine,
Their fair forms sway with ease and grace divine,—
As fair as Venus, each a beauty's queen,
They add new lustre to the brilliant scene;
Like sister nymphs, assembled in a ring,
They throw a gorgeous halo round the king;
Hark to the gushing melodies so fair
That burst upon the sweetly perfumed air;
Such songs as the enchanting siren sings
When harping on the heart's most tender strings:

(SONG)   .

Come fairies fair, join in the dance,
Our noble king with love entrance
And make his heart in rapture dance—
His happiness is ours—

Live while you live ere fall death's shades
Pluck life's sweet flower ere it fades,
Join in the dance, ye glowing maids,
Beguile the fleeting hours.

Long live Belshazzar, mighty king!
'Tis to thy shrine our praise we bring;
May far resounding echoes-ring
With songs of jubilation.
Bright gleams the lustre of thy fame,
Great is the power of thy name,
Thy glory all the world proclaim:
"Belshazzar, king of nations!"

O Babylon, queen of all the world,
Who o'er all thy banner of beauty unfurled,
And thy enemies back to defeat hast hurled,
Thy daughters sing thy glory;

Our tongues shall sing it o'er and o'er
Till to-day be called a day of yore:—
When the songs we sing are heard no more,.
New tongues shall tell thy story.

.

In mellow tones first sing the song,
Sing it through the night so long,
As we lightly dance along,
Softly now were singing,—
Louder still! Our merry tune
Seems to rise above the moon,
And the echoes soon, ah soon,
Shall set creation ringing!

The brilliant lights shine down upon
Young maids whose spring has just begun,
As gay and free as the mermaid's song,
And those whose glass is almost run:

Both old and young are full of glee,—
Old age can not the gayety mar,
For every heart is light and free.—
But o'er them gleams a fatal star!

The tables now are set and they
Are waiting on the guests,
And slaves stand ready to obey
Their sovereign's requests.
Ah! what a treat for one and all;
The fruits and luscious wines—
How bright it sparkles in the cup—
The maid's eyes it outshines!
Ah! yes 'tis sweet before the eye,
It works a mystic thrall:
Alas! how many find too late,
'Tis burning venom, gall!

But as the king sits down to sup,
And sips the nectar from his cup,

Old Satan takes a seat beside,
As though he wished something to say;
But his intention's not to chide,
But instigate him on his way:
"Thou art a great and mighty king,
Free as the eagle on the wing,
Thy fort defies all other castles,
And lordly princes are thy vassals;
On earth there's none can govern thee!
Thy will alone thy guide shall be!"
But conscience whispers, scarcely heard:
"Thou haughty, unrelenting fool,
Since thou hast heaven's king deferred,
Thou must obey the devil's rule!"

Meanwhile they feast and sup and drink,
And louder still the goblets clink:
Some praise their gods of silver, gold,
With words and actions manifold,
While others in their maddened glee

Are tumbling like a surging sea,
Or like a vast and living ocean,
To keep the poetry of motion.

See yonder, dancing with a queen,
The king — 'tis but to plainly seen,
By the expression of his eyne,
That he has drunk the glistening wine,
And now in his riches he thinks he may revel —
But into his mouth he has ushered the devil —
In one of the mildest disguises of Satan —
To rob him of senses, of thoughts and of brains:
Yes, Bacchus is murderer, thief and a villain;
His forehead is branded as sure as was Cain's.

Oh! now if Satan could be heard,
His blood would chill with every word:

"Be happy now O fool, while yet you may,
For soon, too soon, your soul shall pass away,
And ere the breaking of another day,

For help in vain, in vain thou shalt implore;
Beyond death's flood, on the grim and shadowy shore,
Thou shalt remain, my slave forevermore!

"A yawning hell, a terrible abyss
Where fiery, flame-tongued serpents sway and hiss,
And gone for aye is every earthly bliss —
Yes, even now my cavern yawns for thee,
And soon, ah soon, thy captive soul shall be
A victim of th' eternal sulphury sea!

"Ha! ha! ha! ha! thour't tottering on the brink
Of hell itself! What? still another drink?
Ah fool, forge thou thy chain's last fatal link!
Drink on, let not the revelry abate;
Laugh on, thou fool, until I sing thy fate;
Fallen, fallen, fallen is Babylon, the great!

O wine, wine, strangle all his gloomy tho'ts,
Drown consciousness in seas of merry tho'ts
And hide his foe's deep laid and fatal plots;

Choke piping conscience in his very throat:
When on the height of joy, extinguish hope
And let experience in darkness grope!

"Seest in thy merry madness naught but joy?
Ha! ha! 'tis well! on then without alloy;
Thy lease of life is short: thyself enjoy.
Think not, great king, of danger, till too late;
Awake not from thy dream to learn thy fate!
Dance on bright flowers to Inferno's gate.

"O, couldst thou gaze into that chasm below,
Into that murky, lurid, dismal glow,
And see my fettered fiends flit to and fro
Like ghastly shadows of myself, and there
Behold that haggard, woe-bespeaking glare
With which their brine-wrung eyes forever stare!

"These are my foul and blood-bedabbled ghouls,
Whose eyes gleam like eternal glowing coals,
Awaiting Death to bring more damned souls!

They once were kings and princes, dukes and lords;
On earth's great stage as stars they've held the boards,
But now they are with my condemned hordes.

"Be thou a humble beggar or a king,
No odds to me, for from the sea of sin,
In my stout nets, all sorts I gather in.
Ha! ha! ha! ha! I have thee in my grasp,
And now my part is but to hold thee fast,
And mine shall be. the victory at last!"

The orchestra strikes up its strains,—
The rolling drum, the cymbal's jingle
O'erwhelm the voices of the throng
Which with the festive music mingle
And falls upon the quiet night,
Awakes the songsters in the trees
And drives the slumber from their eyes,
As't floats upon the swelling breeze.
And the din grows worse and worse

While the liquor freely flows,
Now a prayer, now a curse,
And the time thus swiftly goes—
But the music gay and light
Is heard by the wary foes
In the silent wake of night,
Where the campfire's dim light glows.

The midnight hour is almost flown
And still Belshazzar holds his throne.

"The raven sought the eagle nest:
Now, in despair seeks peace and rest!
Ha! ha! thus shall it ever be;
The weak must lose the victory—
Ha! ha! ha! ha! be gay and laugh
And to your king the rich wine quaff!
Bring forth," the drunken monarch cries
In voice like thunder from the skies,
"The vessels taken from the shrine

Of Israel's God for they are mine—
Bring forth, — I hold the ruling rods,—
That we may drink unto our gods!
Who dares encroach and say us nay?
None while I live and here hold sway
For every yes and every no
My will dictates is law!"

                      When lo!

A flash of most prognostic light
Illumines now the halls.
Such that the sun ne'er shone so bright
Upon the castle walls!
'T is but a transient flash, again
As lightning it is gone!
An instant is enough to call
Th' attention of the throng.

Who had the mysterious power
Such revelry to stay?

The echo of the roaring din
And tumult dies away.

See, yonder, breaking through the clouds,
The ghastly midnight moon
Glares at the scene of revelry
Which died away so soon.

But ah! how pale and wan she looks,
Then hides behind a cloud:
Why thus withdraw and wrap the world
In midnight's darkest shroud?

Ah! is there not, in heav'n above,
A mystic, unseen pow'r
Who sways the constant nature's laws
To suit the purpose of the hour?

God hides the swift approaching foe
That they may not be seen

Until they enter, armed for war,
Upon the brilliant scene!

That flash the revelry suppressed
And sent a chill through ev'ry breast:
Now all is silent as a grave,
All hush'd as if by death's cold wave
Subdued—

A scarcely whisper'd pray'r
Revives the deathlike calm, then here and there
Among the terror stricken throng
A shriek of frightened women loud and long
The awful silence breaks.—

Again a spell,
And each one's bosom seems to fairly swell
With guilty fears which conscience will not quell;
Accusing conscience will not be suppressed,
But whispers: "Guilt" within each guilty breast.

Behold upon that pale, white wall—
A ghost! a spirit hand in mortal shape;—
As pale as death, as white as snow,
And all must see it — not one can escape!

Belshazzar saw the sudden light,
He turned, beheld the ghastly sight
Upon the wall.   An oath he swore,
And dashed his goblet to the floor:
"What fiend from hell amongst us here
Dares with our banquet interfere?
That black magician to me bring
Who thus has dared to mock his king!
By mighty Jove, that slave shall burn!
My fool his ashes from an urn
Shall scatter at the feet of Bel
Who'll trample him to deepest hell!"

Is it ever treacherous wine
That shapes that awful stain?

Or is it the fantastic work
Of á wild and reeling brain?
Is it despairing madness that
So makes the revellers start?
In heaven's name what else can strike
Such terror to the heart?

There with its finger, thin and white,
It writes upon the wall
With ink of a translucent light
Before the eyes of all!
Is it an evil omen, or
A message to the king?
What are the news this ghastly hand
His majesty would bring?
Is it the hand of death that writes
The message of his doom?
Or is't, perchance, an epitaph
To place above his tomb?
Is it a harbinger of death?

The masses stand and hold their breath:
Ah! certain 'tis 'tis not a dream,
Although to some it thus may seem,
For hundreds saw the self-same sight,—
The silent hand, the blaze of light
Had met a thousand sleepless eyes
And made them start with dread surprise!

The hand of fate still moves and writes—
Then disappears from human sight
As suddenly as it had come!
The silent messenger is gone —
But leaves his message there,
And everyone to stare,
For not a soul could read it!

The monarch trembles and his eyes do start
As though they fain like stars from place would dart;
His countenance is changed, his face grows pale,
His form, so full of strenght, begins to quail;

Despair lends strenght! he hates this dread suspense;
He'll know the worst; he'll pierce this myst'ry dense!
"Ye pow'rs of heav'n and hell, explain, explain!
Are any here who read, read not in vain?
O ye all-seeing prophets, soothsayers, come!
If you have aught to say, remain not dumb!
Ye midnight-piercing hags, ye learned men,
Approach, unveil the message of this pen!
He who unfolds to me the secret tale,
Tears from my eager eyes th' impending veil,
Him shall I make the greatest of my lords,
Wealth, title his, all that my pow'r affords;
In scarlet shall he dress, and wear a chain,
And with myself shall o'er a kingdom reign!"

Thus spoke the aged queen: "Art thou a man?
A soldier who would stand in the battle's van,
Who, beard to beard, would meet the enemy,
Fight like a fiend to death or victory?
And now a shadow makes you quake with fear,

And all your manly instincts disappear!

Thou growest pale as one who is not well!

Come, come, this piping voice of conscience quell;

God grant thee health and life and prosp'rous reign,

And grant that some one may this sight explain.

Look! these Chaldeans stand and gaze as fools,

They cannot read! It is beyond their rules;

Magicians and the pow'rs of hell stand back.

This task is one too great! The brains they lack!

Out on them all, impostors! I know one

Who'll shame them at their own trade! Hark, my son,

Within your kingdom is a man who reads

Mysterious signs, and, seeing fortune's seeds,

Tells if they do possess the power to grow;

If signs like this have any weight or no;

Explains mysterious prophesies and dreams,

And looks into the future's dark extremes:

His name was Daniel, Beltesazar now,

One of the jewish prisoners, I trow.

Astronomers and men of wisdom came

Before the king and sought the wreath of fame;
Chaldean soothsayers with each other vied,
And oracles who nature's laws defied:
Thy father put their genius to the test
But Beltesazar far outshone the rest:
The king, thy father placed him o'er them all!
Have him explain the writing on the wall.
Speak, speak the word and I will have him called!"

Belshazzar listens calmly to the end,
Then bids his mother for the prophet send.
"I will! yes, bring him here without delay;
He shall relieve my heart of this dismay!
O hasten, time, fly swiftly on your wings!"
No! time is not a slave, not e'en to kings!
Swift messengers are sent at once to bring
The learned seer before the anxious king.

The moments pass, each seems a leaden hour
Beneath whose weight the monarch seems to cower.

Ere long, attended by the royal queen,

The prophet Daniel enters on the scene.

The king falls like a subject to his feet,

And thus the learned seer doth he entreat:

"O seer, I'm in distress so great and deep!

My wisest men all fail to answer me

The meaning of this monstrous waking dream;

O give me of the future but a gleam

That I no longer may uncertain be.

Dive, if thou canst, into the secret's sea

And fathom this unnatural mystery.

The king doth offer thee a brother's hand,

And thou shalt be third ruler of the land!

He bows, and thus he speaks unto the king

In voice that makes the silent palace ring:

"O king, thy honored gifts I do decline;

My humble services are ever thine:

Though all thy men of wisdom read in vain,

The writing on yon wall I will explain:

The words are: Mene, Tekel, Upharsin.
Hark! for I will explain what lies therein:
God placed thy father on a dizzy height!
Crowned him with glory, majesty and might,
Gave him the ruling sceptre in his hand
And made him sovereign of a mighty land;
But he, ungrateful for a gift so great,
Abused his pow'r and justly met his fate;
Denied the presence of God's aiding hand
In making him sole ruler of the land;
Insulted and blasphemed his holy name,
And lived in base idolatry and shame;
Whom he desired he bade his vassals kill
And there was none to contradict his will.
He ruled, a tyrant in his royal seat
While humble subjects trembled at his feet:
Great nations bowed before him and revered
A king whose arrogance to heaven reared.
But 'tis no need that I his tale should tell,—
The story of his fall thou knowest well:

God took from him the kingdom that he gave
And placed him lower than the basest slave;
His sole companions were the ox and ass,
The forest his abode, his food was grass:
Thy haughty father lived to sadly learn
The power of Him whose love he dared to spurn;
And thou, his son, still followed in his path —
Not heeding the Inevitable's wrath,
Thou still defied His power, scorned His love,
Yes, hurled defiance to the King above.
Thou hast ignited heaven's wrath for spite,
And heaven's King says it shall burn to-night!
The Lord shall take thy kingdom from thy hand —
A Persian king shall thy successor be,
Grim Death shall on thy forhead place his brand,
And thou more ghastly spirits soon shall see.
On you bright wall of thy last earthly room,
Read, Babylon's king, the record of thy doom!"

Like thunder following the flash
The words of doom fell from the seer: —
New terror wakes on every side,
And every soul is full of fear.

An awful quiet reigns supreme
Upon the scene of mirth, —
An ill forboding stillness as
Precedes a cyclone's birth.
Like statues rooted to the floor,
Pale, haggard, motionless they stand,
Amazed and speechless now as stones, —
Their mind's eye gazing on that hand.

The monarch, trembling listens, — then he starts
As though his mind were pierced with sudden darts;
Imaginary lines begin to form, —
Imaginary battles rage and storm, —
Imagination's ghosts flit to and fro, —-
Anon, he thinks he hears th' approaching foe:

"Methinks I see the glitt'ring weapons flash!
Hark! was not that the saber's hostile clash?
Arm, men, like human devils brave the fight —
Sell life for life for we must die to-night!"

                              But if one chance
To leave the castle for a while,
And towards the river roam,
The still Euphrates, Babylon's Nile,
Where, soft winds sigh and moan,
There's to be seen another sight;
Another army gather'd here, —
Not drunken revelers of the night,
But warriors, earnest and sincere.

Hark! listen to the murmur of the — what?
Is that the thunder from the distant skies?
No! one reflection tells us it is not
Though 'tis as near as one might first surmise;
But 'tis the ill forboding of a storm, —

The clouds with fury threaten soon to burst —
A long and awful night before the morn!
A dreary fight and blood for those who thirst!

Now, while the moon sails out between the clouds
To pierce the darkness with her gentle beams
And lift from earth a moment those dark shrouds,
As if to rob young nature of her dreams,
Behold! upon the dark Euphrates' banks,
Deserted but a few short hours ago,
A formidable phalanx lines it now —
The army of the unexpected foe!

Thus, while they revel in sweet fortune's lap,
The enemy prepare the fatal trap
Through which the king must fall from such a height
Into the dark and unknown cave of night!
They've labored while their victims were at play,
Improved each moment to avoid delay:
The work goes bravely on without a pause —

With patient toil they mean to gain their cause:
In their designs no rash act they employ
Which might the fruits of all their work destroy;
As one man they all work, no effort save
In digging king Belshazzar's early grave!
They work as though their lives depended on
(Perhaps it does) how soon this work is done.
The hour draws nigh when fortune's wheel shall turn
And Babylon her vanity must learn!

Hist! all is quiet,
The work is done
Long ere the rising
Of the sun!

Look! now the river
Has changed its course, —
The mighty current
Has lost its force!

More than rushing, rolling waters,
Scarce a sound is heard;
Something like a distant humming,
But not one plain word:
And the dim lights growing dimmer,
Are not noticed as they glimmer,
But there's an entrance neath the walls
Surrounding Babylon's castle halls!
The way prepared, the massive army halt
While Cyrus gives instructions for th' assault.

"Sleep now, Belshazzar's sentinels,
On Babylon's turret peaks,
Nor wake until ye're in my power!"
Thus now the leader speaks.

"O fools! when fortune's goddess smiles,
Be wary! soon perhaps you'll grieve,
For she is fickle, full of wiles,
And only smiles but to deceive.

"When dazzled, dazed and beastly drunk,
Come death, without a warning,
And make Belshazzar's gayest night
A night without a morning!

"The river, friends, has yielded us a passage:
The greatest obstacle is now removed,
And with God's aid we'll play the rivers's part
And enter neath the walls of Babylon!
Now, when we enter, friends, fear naught within:
Be valiant and fight and we must win:
Consider this: The foes we now shall meet
Are those whom once before we did defeat
When they were sober, wide awake, prepared,
Awaiting our attack with weapons bared,
Their allies by their side upon the field,
And face to face we forced their lines to yield.

We now shall fall upon them unexpected,
At such a time when fiend intoxication
Has muddled many brains and made the victims

Unfit to meet emergencies and danger;
While many are in swinish sleep reposing,
And revellers are merrily carousing,
Ne'er thinking of the peril pending o'er them,
Far from suspecting what to-night's transpired.
When they discover suddenly the danger,
When they behold our army in the city,
Their consternation will outdo itself
And all the more unfit them for the task.

"But, if perchance, they apprehend our plot,
They'll mount upon their places of abode
And hurl death-dealing missiles on our heads
From every side; but have no fear of this,
For fortune is against them even here:
Their houses are of palm-trees built, their walls
Anointed with bitumen all around:
These facts speak boldly in our favour now;
When from their roofs they hurl their missiles down,
Set fire to their dwellings! burn them down!

The people will be forced to leave at once
Or perish for their rashness, in the flames!
Then spread destruction round you far and wide;
The fire-god, Vulcan, fights upon our side!

"Gobryas, now shalt thou our captain be
To lead our forces on to victory,
For thou art best acquainted with the way;
Make no unnecessary, rash delay,
But once within the walls, conduct us straight,
The nearest way unto the palace gate."

He answers thus: "I will! and I've no doubt
But we shall find the palace doors unbarred,
For revelry is holding sway to-night, —
The sentinels most likely drinking hard:
But we must fall upon them suddenly
Lest they detect our plot and be on guard."

"Then march at once! The precious moments fly:
Let not another pass us idly by:
Come, give them not a moment to prepare, —
To-morrow Babylon's wealth the Persians share!"

The soldiers form in solid ranks
Where lately were a river's banks:
Avenging looks this midnight band,
As, sword in girdle, spear in hand,
Stealthily they forward march
Underneath the massive arch,
Swiftly stealing on their prey,
Who, had this been open day,
Might have escaped, but fate said, no!
And heaven would not have it so,
For mighty Babylon's doom was sealed,
As was on that same night revealed.

Within the walls at last, they climb the banks
To learn if they could force the gates of brass
Which boldly face the river on each side:
They yield! and through these passage ways they pass!

King Cyrus sends his faithful spies about
To clear the facts which, shrouded now in doubt,
When brought to light their weakness would expose
And aid them in the capture of their foes.

As one by one the trusty scouts return,
Delivering the news which they could learn,
Shrewd Cyrus builds the ladder to success,
And thus his generals doth he address:

"The palace doors are locked; we can not enter
Unless by stratagem we gain our cause;
We can not wait for sluggard time's assistance —
We must be brief! 'tis danger now to pause!

"Look there, round yonder blazing campfire gathered,
The sentinels, drunk and maddened by the wine,
Enjoying life as kings and not as vassals,
And no more fit for war than muddled swine!

"They'll never think of swift approaching danger,
Nor dream of aught but wine and revelry,
But, merrily carousing, dancing, drinking,
Will prove tame victims for their enemy.

"Gobryas, thou shalt cautiously approach
Yon camp-fire and attack the sentinels there:
Slay some and thus strike terror to them all:
Let cries of terror pierce the midnight air!

Meanwhile, I with Gadatas and his forces
Will march with all haste to the palace gate
(All must be done with the least commotion)
Then we'll surround the entrances and wait.

"When you attack the guards around the fire,
Th' assault will strike such fear to every heart
That they will raise an outcry for assistance;
Then from their pleasant dreams the lords will start!

"The king in haste will open wide the portals
To ascertain the cause of such a din,
And in that dire moment of confusion,
Without delay our soldiers shall rush in!"

These orders given, each force resumes its task,
And hid behind the midnight's raven mask,
In strenght a host, in heart a single man,
They set to work to execute the plan.

They seperate: Gadatas with king Cyrus
On conqueror's wings toward the palace hies,
Gobryas to the camp, as Cyrus ordered,
To raise a panic by his victims' cries.

As silently the armies move along
No sound prevails, save revellers dying song:
All's peaceful silence, now, save here and there
A drunken laughter falls upon the air,
Then all is ominous, still and dark —
Another sound! but oh how different!

Hark!

A cry of terror breaks the awful stillness!
Another follows, then a general wail!
The dreadful plan shall lack no execution!
The awful clamor says it shall not fail!

The palace-doors are suddenly flung open!
The guests rush out! Out? No! it is in vain!
For they are driven back in wild confusion;
The few who gain the open air are slain!

Before us lies the last sad scene:
Not flowers sweet nor forests green,

With rippling waters on a night serene,
But the king's domains again are seen.

The selfsame scene on which our dazzled gaze
Beheld the highest pinnacle of bliss
But few short hours ago: —
Alas, now look what different phase!
Whose hand has changed that scene of happy bliss
To deepest depths of woe?

Fickle fortune's wheel is turned
And ended is the gayety and mirth,
And now the king would gladly give
His kingdom for another day on earth
But no! alas, 't would not be granted,
For now the sins which he had planted
Were ripe and ready reaped to be,
And, sown in sorrow reaped in gladness,
Sown in glory, reap'd in sadness,
O say, what shall the harvest be?

Still fear and anger rage within the king:
Like one who's doomed to fill an early grave,
Of all his self-possession he's deprived;
Accusing conscience has him now a slave:
"Where shall I hide from God almighty's face?
What shall I do? Prepare at once to fly?
Where? No! On earth there is no hiding place —
And heav'n is locked to me — and I must die!

What! Must I die? Who says to me, "Thou must!"
Am I a king? A slave tells me I must,
And bids me tremble! I have men to fight,
Brave soldiers to defend a sovereign's right!
I tremble? No! down, coward conscience, down!
I still possess a kingdom and a crown!"

The chain is forged! O fatal links!
Like death-knells sound the goblets' clinks!
Instead of wines and royal drinks,
The clash of the sabre, the helmets clang,

The blood from the heart-fount, the terrible pang
Felt only when death sticks his poisonous fang
Deep into his victim to seek for his life!
The battle-spear, saber, the lance and the knife
Play their terrible parts in the fight for life:
Great crimson floods reek on the floor,
And everywhere are stains of gore;
And in the light that gloated o'er
That horrid sight the weapons gleam
While frightened women fly and scream
As though awakened from a dream!
And sadly swells the dying groan,
Hearts anguish-riven wail and moan,
Air castles to the air are blown!

Belshazzar, full of fear and rage,
Like a fearful demon stands,
He fiercely howls: "I am your king!
Obey ye my commands!"

His hair stands like the lions mane,
His eyes glare as the sun!
He knows the curtain soon must drop —
His part is almost done!

"No hope for bloodless peace remains
And mercy's hour is past!
Escape is vain, but lose or gain,
The die must now be cast!

"Imagination shows two fates —
To die, or live a slave!
Arouse, ye fools and fight like fiends
Or fill a coward's grave!

"Upon the cowards! Drive them back
To their mothers' breasts again
Or smear our sabers with their blood!
Like dogs let them be slain!"

The soldiers hear and rush to war,
The battle trumpets sound,
And in the conflict's roar and din
The monarch's voice is drowned.

The lightning flashes from the swords:
The soldiers fight pell-mell:
If they must die by Persian hands,
Their lives they'll dearly sell.

Like brutal beasts and not like men
They meet and fight the foe
As hand to hand and beard to beard
They strike the fatal blow:

They scatter dead and dying side by side —
Belshazzar's throne with blood is deeply dyed!

But look into the thickest of the fight!
The king, with enemies to left and right,

With wrinkled brow and fearful, angry mien
. Stands like one 'wakened from a hideous dream.

At last the monarch draws his sword to kill;
He'd fain escape but fights against his will:
All hope within his bosom now is dead,
And on his brow are marks of fear and dread.
His hope is gone — experience is left, —
But what is day when of a sun bereft?
All dark despair, no vision of a heaven;
Therefore, in death, his soul is anguish-riven!
No hope for earthly bliss; that awful hand
Had grasped that hope that was so bright and grand!
The guiding star of life torn from his sky,
He rushes to destruction — he must die.

With maddened frenzy he pursues the fight
His men are slain before his very eyes;
His madness still increases at the sight —
And all the world in anger he defies.

The fight grows hot, the arrows fly around
The king and threaten to fulfill his doom:
The dying groan blends with the helmet's sound;
Ah, many homes will now be filled with gloom.

Alas! Belshazzar's bound by Bachus' chains;
But still he fights, and every nerve he strains,
To gain again possession of his mind;
Confused with fear and rage, like brute that's blind,
He sees no friend but strikes both friend and foe,
And though he weakens at each serveral blow,
His weapon meets his enemy's and wards
Off blow by blow — Alas! he's off his guard!
His actions fail! his enemy's point is pressed
Against his heart, now — buried in his breast!
An awful shriek — a smother'd cry of pain,
And then he seems to see his glory wane.

"O death! wouldst thou convey a soul to hell?
Alas! my kingdom, life and all, farewell!"

A smothered curse is cast upon the air,
The last word uttered in his deep despair.

He tries to raise his sword again — in vain:
He writhes and shows deep signs of heavy pain:
Ah, sweet revenge! so near — and yet so far!
Yes, out of reach; his foe he can not mar.
His eyes afire — for blood they seem to thirst.
His bosom heaves as though it fain would burst; —
Death steps before him with his poisonous dart
To help him on his dreary journey start:

The ferry-man is waiting at the boat
For him that he may set his craft afloat,
Awaiting but the capture of his ghost
To waft him o'er to Pluto's dreary coast.

Perhaps the king now sees his awful fate —
Alas! too well, yes too well, and — too late!

He stands a moment as in dread suspense —
As though, if death approach, to brave defence!

He feels death's cold hand reach to clog his throat!
He seems to see grim Satan grin and gloat!
He gathers all his strength and powers of will,
Strains every nerve to shake that awful chill:

In vain! in vain! That grasp grows firm and fast!
An everlasting prisoner at last!
He staggers, falls in agony of death,
And struggles still in vain to gain his breath;
Death rattles in his throat; he's sinking fast —
The shades of death his wrinkled brow o'ercast;
Cold death has almost frozen every vein
And still he strives to raise his head again!
His pale lips quiver — ah, perhaps he tries
To bid a kingdom for a life — he dies!

"No! down to deepest hell thou sinking wreck!
Ten thousand kingdoms can not buy thee back!
Thus far thou goest, now the word is "Stay!"
Thy cup of life must now be ta'en away
And handed to another with thy crown;
Fools drink their cup too suddenly and drown!
Go! join thy fellow-revellers in sin
Ha! ha! ha! ha! Thus do I rake them in!"

Prostrate he lies, his body is asleep:
Ah what a slumber, awful, heavy, deep!
The sun that sank shall never show its light,
For this begins a dark, uncertain night,
A night of dreams, O, who can tell what dreams
But he who sleeps, till doomsday's bright sunbeams
Shall break the night of death when time is past
And scatter all dark shades which death had cast?
When the veil of night's forever drawn aside
And the portals of the morning open wide,
O, will not all the dreams of death come true

And then present themselves in brighter view?
Will then Belshazzar start from out that sleep,
With trembling fear, lest dreams their promise keep,
To hear above all other noise and din
That awful; Mene! Tekel! Upharsin!

No matter! long he's rested 'neath the sod
And to an unknown land his soul has flown;
Whate'er his fate, leave to the Judge above;
Its secret depths no mortal's ever known.

A Median king sits on th' Assyrian's throne; —
The king that was — where's he? look! dead as stone,
There at his feet, with dim and upturned eyes,
Cold, blood-bespattered, dead, Belshazzar lies!
His doom's fulfilled! The battle's lost and won!
The curtain drops, the tragedy is done.

—◦◦ FINIS. ◦◦—